The Let Them Now Theory Journal

A Step-by-Step Self-Help Interactive Guide to Letting Go and Moving Forward

A WORKBOOK

Elysia Evarista

© 2024 by Elysia Evarista

All rights reserved.

No part of this book may be reproduced, stored in a retrieval system, or transmitted in any form or by any means, electronic, mechanical, photocopying, recording, or otherwise, without the prior written permission of the author, except as provided by United States copyright law.

The information in this book is for educational and informational purposes only. While every effort has been made to ensure the accuracy of the information provided, the author makes no representations or warranties regarding the completeness, accuracy, or reliability of any information, or the outcome of any strategies or techniques discussed.

Disclaimer:

The content provided in The Let Them Now Theory Journal: A Step-by-Step Self-Help Interactive Guide to Letting Go and Moving Forward is for informational and educational purposes only. The author is not a licensed therapist, medical professional, or counselor. This journal is not intended to diagnose, treat, or replace professional advice from a healthcare provider.

Readers are encouraged to seek professional guidance and support when necessary. The author and publisher do not assume any liability for any outcomes or consequences that arise from following the suggestions or strategies provided in this book.

By using this journal, readers acknowledge and agree that they are responsible for their own actions and decisions.

Introduction

Overview of The Let Them Theory

Introduction to the Concept: The Power of Two Words

At its core, The Let Them Theory is a revolutionary guide that centers on the simplicity and transformative power of two words: "Let Them." These words form the foundation for a philosophy that empowers individuals to let go of control, reduce emotional burdens, and refocus on what truly matters—themselves. This theory is not about apathy or indifference but about reclaiming personal agency, freeing oneself from the exhausting cycle of trying to manage others' opinions, reactions, and behaviors.

Mel Robbins, celebrated for her relatable and science-backed insights, presents this theory as a gateway to happiness, fulfillment, and resilience. Rooted in psychology, neuroscience, and personal experience, the book offers a practical framework for anyone feeling overwhelmed, stuck, or disconnected from their goals and relationships.

Why It's a Game-Changer

Millions of readers resonate with The Let Them Theory because it tackles universal struggles:

- The tendency to overthink and overmanage.
- The fear of being judged or misunderstood.
- The exhaustion that comes from trying to control what's outside our power.

The theory empowers readers to:

Shift focus inward—towards self-love, self-fulfillment, and authentic happiness.

Embrace freedom from external expectations, drama, and judgment.

Simplify their mental load by releasing the need to fix or manage others.

By applying these principles, readers can build healthier relationships, overcome self-doubt, and create a life aligned with their true desires.

Structure and Approach

The book is divided into three major sections with actionable insights, personal anecdotes, and expert-backed strategies:

Part 1: The Let Them Theory

This foundational section introduces the core philosophy and sets the stage for practical implementation.

Chapter 1: Stop Wasting Your Life on Things You Can't Control

Robbins explains how much energy we waste on the uncontrollable, urging readers to reclaim their focus and sanity.

Chapter 2: Getting Started: Let Them + Let Them

A step-by-step guide to applying "Let Them" in daily life, emphasizing mindset shifts and intentional living.

Part 2: You and the Let Them Theory

This section focuses on personal growth and resilience in the face of common emotional challenges:

Managing Stress:

Life's inevitability of stress is explored with tools to reframe and manage it.

Fearing Other People's Opinions:

Robbins delves into the paralyzing effects of judgment and provides ways to overcome them.

Dealing with Emotional Reactions of Others:

Strategies to maintain peace when others project their emotions or lash out.

Overcoming Chronic Comparison:

A reframing of comparison as a tool for growth rather than a source of inadequacy.

Each chapter includes insights from psychology, relatable stories, and practical exercises to help readers reframe their thoughts and behavior patterns.

Part 3: Your Relationships and the Let Them Theory

This section addresses the relational dimensions of the Let Them Theory, offering transformative tools for friendships, partnerships, and family dynamics.

Mastering Adult Friendship: How to deepen, sustain, or gracefully release friendships.

Motivating Others to Change: Guidance on inspiring rather than controlling others.

Helping Struggling Loved Ones: A compassionate approach to providing support without overstepping.

Choosing the Love You Deserve: Empowering readers to cultivate romantic relationships built on authenticity and mutual respect.

Key Themes and Takeaways

Control is an Illusion:

The Let Them Theory drives home the idea that trying to control others' opinions, emotions, or actions is futile and self-destructive. By letting go, we create space for peace and joy.

Boundaries are Empowering:

The book emphasizes the importance of setting boundaries—both for ourselves and others—to foster healthier connections and protect mental health.

Embrace Vulnerability and Authenticity:

Through her personal stories and those of others, Robbins inspires readers to let go of perfectionism and embrace their true selves.

Resilience Through Reframing:

Whether dealing with judgment, rejection, or comparison, the book teaches readers how to reframe challenges as opportunities for growth.

The Let Them Theory is more than just a guide; it's a mindset that can be applied in every aspect of life—from parenting and romantic relationships to professional and social interactions. The conclusion ties all the lessons together, urging readers to embrace the power of "Let Them" as an everyday tool for living a free, fulfilled, and intentional life.

The appendix provides additional insights on how to apply the theory in specific contexts, such as:

- Parenting
- Team dynamics
- School settings
- Romantic relationships
- Family interactions

Why This Book Matters

In a world where everyone seems burdened by overthinking, social comparison, and emotional overwhelm, The Let Them Theory offers a timely solution. With its accessible language, science-backed approach, and actionable strategies, this book has the potential to transform lives, relationships, and mindsets—one "Let Them" at a time.

How to Use This Workbook

Welcome to the Let Them Theory Workbook! This companion guide is designed to help you apply the transformative principles of Mel Robbins' The Let Them Theory to your daily life. By diving into the exercises, reflections, and practical tools in this workbook, you'll uncover powerful insights about yourself, strengthen your relationships, and reclaim control over your happiness and goals.

Step-by-Step Guide to Using This Workbook

1. Start with the Book

While this workbook can stand alone, it works best as a companion to The Let Them Theory. If you haven't read the book yet, take some time to do so. Familiarize yourself with the main ideas, stories, and lessons that Mel Robbins shares. This will provide context and inspiration for the exercises in the workbook.

2. Go Chapter by Chapter

This workbook mirrors the structure of The Let Them Theory, with dedicated sections for each chapter. For each subchapter, you'll find:

Summary: A brief recap of the key concepts and ideas.

5 Key Lessons: Important takeaways to reinforce the chapter's message.

4 Self-Reflection Questions: Thought-provoking prompts to help you explore your feelings, beliefs, and behaviors.

Life-Changing Exercises: Practical actions and techniques to help you implement the "Let Them" mindset in real-life situations.

Take your time with each section, and don't rush. Growth happens when you reflect deeply and apply the lessons in meaningful ways.

3. Make It Personal

Use this workbook as a space for honesty and vulnerability. Write freely and authentically—this is your journey. You don't need perfect answers or polished reflections. The goal is to uncover truths, challenge assumptions, and take actionable steps toward change.

4. Track Your Progress

As you move through the workbook, keep track of your progress and revisit earlier sections to see how far you've come. Celebrate small wins, and recognize the positive shifts in your mindset and behavior.

5. Use the Exercises Daily

The exercises in this workbook are designed to be practical and actionable. Whether it's practicing letting go of control, reframing comparisons, or strengthening friendships, these exercises can be integrated into your daily routine. Consistency is key to lasting change.

6. Revisit as Needed

The principles of The Let Them Theory are lifelong tools. Life will present new challenges and opportunities to practice letting go. Return to this workbook whenever you feel stuck, overwhelmed, or in need of a mindset reset.

Workbook Tips for Success

Be Patient with Yourself: Change takes time. If certain concepts or exercises feel challenging, that's okay. Growth is a process.

Stay Open-Minded: Some lessons may feel counterintuitive at first. Give yourself permission to explore and experiment with new ways of thinking.

Share Your Journey: If you feel comfortable, discuss what you're learning with a trusted friend, partner, or support group. Sharing insights can deepen your understanding and provide accountability.

Celebrate Your Wins: Every step forward, no matter how small, is worth celebrating. Acknowledge your efforts and progress along the way.

Your Journey Starts Here

This workbook is more than just a tool; it's your personal guide to transforming how you think about control, relationships, and personal power. By working through each chapter, reflecting on your experiences, and applying the exercises, you'll unlock new levels of freedom, confidence, and joy.

Get ready to embrace the power of "Let Them" and create the life you deserve. Let's get started!

Part One: The Let Them Theory

1. Stop Wasting Your Life on Things You Can't Control

Subchapter Summary

This section focuses on how to stop spending time and energy on things you can't control, which is a major cause of stress, frustration, and burnout. Often, we are overwhelmed by the opinions of others, societal pressures, and uncontrollable circumstances. This leads to feelings of being stuck, resentful, and disconnected from our true desires. The first step to breaking free from this cycle is realizing that the key to happiness and progress lies in focusing only on what is within our control. By learning to "Let Them," we reclaim our energy, reduce stress, and begin focusing on what truly matters: ourselves and our goals.

5 Key Lessons

Control vs. Influence: Recognize the difference between things you can control (your actions, responses, thoughts) and things you can only influence (other people's behaviors, external events).

Energy Conservation: When we focus on what we can control, we conserve emotional energy and reduce the stress of trying to change things that are outside our reach.

Releasing the Need for Approval: Letting go of the need for external validation allows us to stop seeking approval from others and shift our focus back to our own goals and happiness.

Setting Boundaries: By defining what you will and won't tolerate, you can set healthier boundaries without feeling guilty. This creates space for personal growth and well-being.

The Power of Letting Go: The more you practice letting go of uncontrollable aspects of life, the more peace and clarity you experience. This release allows you to move forward with purpose and confidence.

4 Self-Reflection Questions

What are the top three things in my life that I spend the most time and energy trying to control?

How do these uncontrollable things impact my mental and emotional well-being?

How can I start shifting my focus to the areas I can control, like my reactions and decisions?

When was the last time I felt free from external pressure? What did that freedom feel like?

Life-Changing Exercises

Energy Reset: Take a moment to reflect on the energy you're putting into things you can't control. Write them down and consciously choose one area to let go of today. How can you shift your focus to what you can control in that situation?

Boundary Mapping: Draw two columns: one for your personal boundaries and one for areas where you've been letting others cross those boundaries. What needs to change to protect your energy? Start by setting a small, actionable boundary in one area of your life today.

Mindset Shift Exercise: Practice saying "Let Them" aloud whenever you feel yourself getting caught up in someone else's opinion or behavior. Write down three situations where you will actively apply this mindset shift in the coming week.

Reflection on Control: Each night, take five minutes to write down one thing that you tried to control that didn't work out, and then reframe it: What did I learn from letting go of that? How did it change my perspective or actions moving forward?

2. Getting Started: Let Them + Let Them

Subchapter Summary

In this section, we delve into the practical application of the core concept of "Let Them" and how it serves as a tool for taking control of your life. The phrase "Let Them" is a powerful reminder to stop trying to control what you can't and to start focusing on what's within your power. It's not just about letting go of other people's behaviors or opinions, but also about releasing your own inner pressures and self-judgment. For many of us, self-doubt and the desire to please others hold us back. "Let Them + Let Them" teaches you how to shift your mindset in two important ways: let others be who they are, and let yourself be who you are without the need for external approval. This process helps you reclaim your sense of self, reduce stress, and take meaningful steps toward your goals without being bogged down by external pressures.

5 Key Lessons

Releasing Control Over Others: Understand that you can't control how others behave or what they think of you. Once you accept this, you free up your energy to focus on what truly matters—your own actions and decisions.

Empowerment through Self-Acceptance: The more you let go of your self-criticism and the need for validation, the more empowered and confident you become in following your own path.

The Dual Power of "Letting Them": "Let them be who they are" means accepting others for who they are without judgment. "Let them" also applies to yourself—allow yourself to be imperfect, to make mistakes, and to grow at your own pace.

Letting Go of Perfectionism: Stop holding yourself to unattainable standards. By letting go of the need to be perfect, you can create a life that's authentic, fulfilling, and true to your own values.

Building Resilience through Boundaries: Setting healthy boundaries by using the "Let Them" mindset gives you the mental space to bounce back from challenges and build resilience against external stressors.

4 Self-Reflection Questions

What parts of my life do I struggle to "Let Them" in? (For example, am I trying to change my partner's behavior, or seeking approval from my boss?)

How often do I feel pressured to act or be a certain way to fit in with others' expectations? How does this affect my well-being?

What would my life look like if I let others be themselves and allowed myself to fully embrace my true self without judgment?

How can I practice "Letting Them" today in my relationships and personal growth? Which specific situation can I start with?

Life-Changing Exercises

"Let Them" Declaration: Write a letter to yourself where you declare one area of your life where you've been trying to control others or seeking validation. Acknowledge this pattern and commit to letting go. Then, create a specific plan for what you'll focus on instead, based on your own values and desires.

Empathy Practice: Identify someone in your life whose behavior or opinions you've been trying to control or change. Write down one way you can begin to "Let Them" by accepting them as they are. Try this for a week and reflect on how it feels to release judgment.

Self-Compassion Exercise: Whenever you feel the urge to criticize or judge yourself, pause and write down one positive affirmation. Remind yourself that you are enough as you are. Practice this exercise daily for the next week.

Perfectionism Release: Create a list of things you've been holding yourself to perfectionist standards for. Circle one item, then write down three steps you can take to let go of the need for perfection in this area and embrace progress over perfection.

Part Two: You and The Let Them Theory

Managing Stress

3. Shocker: Life Is Stressful
Subchapter Summary

In this subchapter, we face the reality that life, in its complexity, is inherently stressful. Whether it's the demands of work, the pressures of relationships, or the constant stream of information and distractions in the modern world, stress is an inevitable part of life. However, this doesn't mean that we have to let it control us. By embracing the "Let Them" mindset, we can navigate stress with greater ease and less overwhelm. The key to managing stress isn't eliminating it, but learning how to respond to it effectively. This subchapter helps you shift your perspective, move from feeling powerless in the face of stress to feeling empowered, and provides strategies for maintaining balance and clarity even when life feels chaotic.

5 Key Lessons

Stress Is a Natural Part of Life: Life will always have its challenges and stressors. Accepting stress as a natural part of the human experience helps you stop fighting against it and start managing it more effectively.

Control Your Response, Not the Situation: While you can't control external circumstances, you do have control over how you respond to them. The "Let Them" theory teaches you to focus on your response, empowering you to approach stress with calm and intention.

The Role of Boundaries in Stress Management: One of the biggest sources of stress comes from not setting or maintaining healthy boundaries. By practicing the "Let Them" mindset, you create emotional space to protect your peace and reduce overwhelm.

Stress and Perfectionism Go Hand-in-Hand: Perfectionism fuels stress. Striving to meet unrealistic standards often leads to burnout. By letting go of the need to be perfect, you alleviate a significant source of unnecessary stress.

Embracing Stress as a Signal: Stress isn't always negative. It can signal that something important needs your attention, whether it's setting boundaries, shifting priorities, or addressing an unmet need. Learning to view stress as a guide instead of an enemy can shift your entire approach to it.

4 Self-Reflection Questions

What situations or people in my life consistently cause me stress? How have I been trying to control or change these situations, and how is this contributing to my stress?

_____
_____
_____
_____
_____
_____
_____
_____
_____
_____
_____
_____
_____
_____

How do I typically react to stress? Do I try to fix everything around me, or do I take a moment to focus on my response to the situation?

What would happen if I accepted stress as a part of life and focused instead on managing my reaction to it? How would this change my experience?

Where do I need to set better boundaries in my life to reduce stress and protect my well-being? What would it look like to say "Let them" in this area?

Life-Changing Exercises

Stress Mapping Exercise: Take a moment to write down the three biggest sources of stress in your life right now. For each, identify the aspects that you can control and the aspects you can't. Then, write down one action you can take to manage your response to the parts you can't control.

Boundary Practice: Pick one area of your life (work, family, friendships, etc.) where you feel overwhelmed. Set a clear boundary (e.g., no answering work emails after 7 PM) and practice saying "Let them" to any pressure or guilt that may arise. Track how this changes your stress level and emotional state.

Perfectionism Release: Reflect on one task or area of your life where you tend to push for perfection. Let go of the need to do it perfectly by setting a realistic goal for progress instead. Celebrate completing the task without stressing over every detail.

Stress Reframe: The next time you feel stressed, pause and ask yourself: "What is this stress trying to tell me?" Use this as an opportunity to reframe your perspective and see stress as a signal to pay attention to your needs or reassess your boundaries.

4. Let Them Stress You Out

Subchapter Summary

In this subchapter, we confront the reality that stress isn't something we can always avoid or control. Sometimes, the stress comes from external sources: other people's actions, societal expectations, and the demands placed upon us. The core message of this chapter is liberating—Let them stress you out. Instead of trying to control other people's behavior, expectations, or reactions, we take a step back and allow others to be who they are, free from our attempts to fix or change them. This mindset shift is empowering because it frees you from the exhausting cycle of trying to control everyone and everything around you. Instead, you focus on managing your own reactions, which is the only part you can truly control. By applying the "Let Them" theory to stress caused by others, you begin to feel more centered, at peace, and in control of your emotional world.

5 Key Lessons

External Stress Is Unavoidable: People, situations, and circumstances will always create stress. Rather than resisting this, embrace the idea that external stress is a part of life, and focus on managing your response to it rather than trying to change it.

You Can't Control Others, But You Can Control Your Reactions: The people around you may act in ways that stress you out, but you have the power to choose how you react. The "Let Them" mindset helps you stop taking on the responsibility of their actions and frees you from being emotionally hijacked.

Stress from Others Is Often About Their Expectations, Not Yours: Many times, we feel stressed because we are trying to meet someone else's expectations—whether it's a boss, family member, or friend. Learning to "Let Them" manage their own expectations of you can release a great deal of unnecessary stress.

Boundaries Protect Your Peace: Letting others stress you out often occurs when you don't set clear boundaries. Establishing boundaries is a powerful way to protect your emotional well-being, ensuring that other people's stress doesn't overrun your life.

Stress as a Mirror for Self-Reflection: When someone stresses you out, instead of blaming them, use it as a tool for self-reflection. Ask yourself why you're reacting the way you are. What unmet need or fear is being triggered? This can lead to valuable insights into your values and emotional triggers.

4 Self-Reflection Questions

Who in my life regularly stresses me out, and what is it about their behavior or expectations that causes me to feel this way?

How can I separate my emotional state from other people's actions or moods? What would it look like if I allowed them to handle their stress without trying to fix it for them?

In what areas of my life do I feel the pressure to meet other people's expectations? How can I practice saying "Let them" in these situations?

When I feel stressed by others, what can I do to pause and reflect on my own emotional response? What is this stress telling me about my boundaries or personal needs?

Life-Changing Exercises

Let Them Stress You Out Exercise: Identify one person in your life who tends to cause you stress. Write down the ways you try to manage or control their behavior (e.g., trying to solve their problems, adjusting your own plans to make them happy). Then, practice saying to yourself, "Let them" as a way of releasing the need to control them. Reflect on how this shift affects your stress level and emotional well-being.

Boundary Setting Practice: Pick a situation where you regularly feel stressed by someone else (e.g., a co-worker's demanding emails or a family member's expectations). Set a clear boundary around this—whether it's a time limit, a communication preference, or a personal need. Write down how it feels to enforce this boundary and how the stress decreases when you take back control of your emotional space.

Stress-Free Interaction: The next time you find yourself stressed by someone's actions or words, consciously detach from their stress. Take a few deep breaths and focus on your own feelings instead of trying to fix the situation. Observe what happens when you stop trying to manage the other person's stress and just focus on managing your own emotional state.

Expectations Check: Think about an area where you feel like you're not meeting someone else's expectations. Write down how this pressure affects your stress. Now, write out how you could shift your mindset to focus on your own expectations instead. Practice redirecting your energy toward your goals and needs rather than trying to meet theirs.

5. Let Them Think Bad Thoughts About You
Subchapter Summary

In this powerful subchapter, we tackle one of the most pervasive sources of stress and self-doubt: the fear of what others think. Many people waste an immense amount of energy worrying about how they are perceived, especially when it comes to negative judgments. The "Let Them" mindset encourages you to release the burden of needing everyone to approve of you or see you in a positive light. You cannot control how others think, and trying to do so only keeps you stuck in a cycle of self-criticism and insecurity. Instead, you are invited to embrace the reality that people will form opinions about you, and that's okay. By letting go of the need for constant validation, you free yourself to live authentically and focus on what truly matters: your own happiness and self-worth. This shift is liberating and allows you to let go of the emotional weight of other people's opinions.

5 Key Lessons

You Can't Control Others' Thoughts: The first step in embracing the "Let Them" mindset is acknowledging that you have no control over how people think about you. Trying to manipulate others' opinions is exhausting and ultimately fruitless. Accepting this liberates you from the constant need to seek approval.

Fear of Judgment is Often Exaggerated: Most of the time, the fear of being judged negatively by others is far greater in our minds than it is in reality. People are often too busy with their own lives to think much about you, and the judgments they do make are a reflection of their own experiences and insecurities, not yours.

Your Self-Worth Shouldn't Depend on Others: True confidence comes from within. When your self-worth is dependent on external validation, it's unstable and fragile. Learning to "Let Them" think what they want frees you to build a solid foundation of self-esteem that doesn't rely on the approval of others.

Opinions are Often Unfounded or Misguided: People often form opinions based on limited information or personal biases. These opinions are not a reflection of your true value. Letting go of the need to correct or defend yourself against such judgments can be an empowering act of self-acceptance.

Focus on the People Who Matter: There will always be people who judge or criticize, but there are also people who support, love, and appreciate you for who you are. By letting go of negative opinions, you can focus on the people whose thoughts truly matter—those who lift you up and help you grow.

4 Self-Reflection Questions

Who in my life have I been overly concerned about pleasing or gaining approval from? How has this affected my emotional well-being and personal growth?

When I fear that others think badly of me, what specific thoughts or behaviors am I trying to change in order to gain their approval? How can I shift my focus from their opinions to my own values and goals?

How does my need for approval from others hold me back from being authentic and true to myself? What would my life look like if I let go of the need for external validation?

Who are the people whose opinions truly matter to me? How can I spend more time nurturing relationships with those who uplift and support me?

Life-Changing Exercises

Let Them Think Exercise: Think of one person in your life whose opinion of you has been causing you stress or self-doubt. Write down the negative thoughts or judgments you imagine they might have about you. Now, practice saying, "Let them think what they want," and feel the weight of their judgment lift off your shoulders. Reflect on how it feels to release this burden.

Self-Worth Affirmations: Write down 5-10 positive affirmations that remind you of your worth, independent of others' opinions. These might include statements like, "I am enough just as I am," "I don't need approval to be valuable," or "I am worthy of love and respect." Repeat these affirmations daily to build a foundation of self-esteem that isn't reliant on external validation.

The Judgment-Free Zone: For the next 48 hours, practice letting go of the need for approval in every situation. Whether you're at work, with friends, or in public, pay attention to how often you catch yourself seeking validation. Consciously remind yourself, "Let them think what they want," and see how this alters your experience. Write about the moments when you felt free from judgment and the emotional relief it provided.

Positive Validation Circle: Reach out to a few close friends or family members who genuinely support you. Share with them something you're proud of about yourself and ask for positive feedback. Let their love and affirmation remind you of who you truly are, and use this as a reminder to seek validation from those who uplift you, not from everyone.

6. How to Love Difficult People
Subchapter Summary

One of the greatest challenges in relationships is dealing with people who are difficult or draining. These individuals can be controlling, critical, or simply hard to please, leaving you feeling frustrated, exhausted, and powerless. In this subchapter, we explore how the "Let Them" mindset can transform your approach to difficult people. Instead of trying to change them or exhaust yourself with emotional battles, you'll learn how to accept their behavior without taking it personally. The "Let Them" approach allows you to establish emotional boundaries, protect your energy, and interact with difficult people from a place of calm and compassion. Loving difficult people doesn't mean accepting bad behavior—it means choosing how you respond and creating space for peace and understanding without sacrificing your self-worth or happiness.

5 Key Lessons

You Can't Change Other People: The first step in loving difficult people is accepting that you cannot control or change their behavior. This realization allows you to stop trying to fix or "correct" them and instead focus on how you can best handle the situation without being emotionally affected.

Don't Take It Personally: Often, difficult people act out due to their own unresolved issues or insecurities. Their behavior is more about them than it is about you. When you stop taking their actions personally, you free yourself from the emotional weight they impose.

Set Boundaries with Compassion: Loving difficult people doesn't mean tolerating toxic behavior. Instead, it means setting clear, healthy boundaries while still maintaining respect and empathy. Establishing boundaries ensures that you can protect your emotional well-being without resorting to anger or resentment.

Respond Instead of Reacting: When faced with challenging people, the key is to respond with calm and thoughtfulness rather than reacting impulsively. The "Let Them" mindset empowers you to stay grounded and not get swept up in their negativity. By practicing self-control, you can approach difficult situations with more compassion and less emotional turmoil.

Choose Peace Over Perfection: It's impossible to please everyone, especially difficult people. The goal isn't to win their approval or try to "fix" their behavior, but to find peace within yourself. By letting go of the need to be right or control the situation, you create space for inner peace and emotional resilience.

4 Self-Reflection Questions

Think of a difficult person in your life. How has their behavior affected your emotional well-being? How have you tried to change or control them in the past?

_____

_____

_____

_____

_____

_____

_____

_____

_____

_____

_____

_____

_____

_____

_____

_____

When dealing with difficult people, how often do you find yourself taking things personally? How can you practice detaching from their behavior and focusing on your own emotional response?

What are some boundaries you need to set with challenging individuals in your life? How can you implement these boundaries in a respectful, compassionate way?

How do you typically respond to difficult people—do you react emotionally or do you pause and respond thoughtfully? How can you start shifting from reaction to response in your interactions?

Life-Changing Exercises

Practice Compassionate Detachment: Choose one person in your life who is difficult to interact with. Practice viewing their actions from a place of compassion rather than judgment. Try to understand their behavior as a reflection of their own struggles and not as a personal attack. Journal about how this shift in perspective changes your emotional response to them.

Set One Boundary: Identify a boundary that you need to set with someone who is difficult. Write down the boundary clearly and confidently, then take action by communicating it to the person. Notice how it feels to assert your needs and protect your emotional well-being.

Pause and Respond: The next time you encounter a difficult situation with someone, consciously pause before reacting. Take a deep breath, reflect on how you want to respond from a place of calm and control, and then respond thoughtfully. Afterward, journal about the experience—how did it feel to maintain control over your emotional response?

Forgiveness Exercise: Think of a difficult person you're holding onto anger or resentment toward. Take a moment to write a letter (which you don't need to send) where you express your feelings of hurt or frustration. Then, write a section where you consciously choose to forgive them, understanding that their actions are not a reflection of your worth. Let go of the burden of holding onto this anger and feel the emotional release that comes with forgiveness.

Dealing with Someone Else's Emotional Reactions

7. When Grown-ups Throw Tantrums
Subchapter Summary

It's easy to assume that tantrums are a behavior confined to children, but adults can throw tantrums too—often in ways that are more subtle, but just as disruptive. These "grown-up tantrums" can range from passive-aggressive comments, emotional outbursts, and silent treatments to manipulative behaviors aimed at gaining control or attention. For many readers, dealing with such behaviors can be incredibly draining and frustrating. In this subchapter, we explore how the "Let Them" mindset can help you manage these situations without getting sucked into the drama or losing your own peace of mind. By recognizing the underlying emotions behind adult tantrums, you'll learn to protect yourself from being manipulated or overwhelmed while still maintaining a sense of empathy. The key is not to take it personally and to focus on responding with emotional maturity, rather than reacting emotionally. Letting go of the need to fix or control the situation allows you to remain centered, no matter how others behave.

5 Key Lessons

Adult Tantrums Are About Control, Not You: When someone throws a tantrum, whether through yelling, silence, or manipulation, it's often a way for them to regain control or assert dominance. Understanding that their behavior is not a reflection of your worth allows you to detach emotionally from their actions and not take it personally.

Don't Engage in the Drama: Adult tantrums thrive on reaction. When you engage in the drama—whether by arguing, defending yourself, or trying to fix things—you only fuel the behavior. The "Let Them" mindset encourages you to step back, resist the urge to react, and create space for calm.

Empathy Over Emotion: It's easy to become defensive or angry when someone throws a tantrum, but practicing empathy can help you respond from a place of understanding rather than frustration. Recognize that the person's behavior is often a result of their own unresolved emotions or insecurity, not something inherently wrong with you.

Set Boundaries with Respect: While it's important to let others have their emotional moments, it's equally crucial to set boundaries that protect your well-being. You don't have to tolerate poor behavior. Setting respectful boundaries allows you to maintain your emotional health and prevents you from being dragged into their emotional chaos.

Don't Take the Bait: The goal is to stay calm and composed, even when someone is attempting to provoke or manipulate you. Adult tantrums often involve triggering emotions like guilt, shame, or anger. By recognizing the tactic and staying grounded, you avoid being baited into an emotional confrontation, which only escalates the situation.

4 Self-Reflection Questions

Think about a recent situation where an adult in your life threw a tantrum. How did you react? How might you have responded differently if you had applied the "Let Them" mindset?

How does it feel to be the target of an adult's emotional outburst or tantrum? What specific emotions or triggers do you notice arise in you during these moments?

What boundaries do you need to set with individuals who regularly throw tantrums? How can you enforce these boundaries with respect and without guilt?

Reflect on a time when you witnessed someone else managing a tantrum or emotional outburst effectively. What strategies did they use that you could apply in your own life?

Life-Changing Exercises

Empathy Practice: Next time someone throws a tantrum or becomes emotionally volatile around you, take a moment to pause and practice empathy. Instead of focusing on their behavior, try to understand what emotional needs or insecurities are driving their actions. Afterward, journal about how it felt to approach the situation with compassion rather than frustration.

Tantrum-Response Role-Play: Identify a person who tends to throw tantrums and role-play how you would respond with emotional maturity. Practice keeping a calm and composed demeanor while setting healthy boundaries. Rehearse these responses until they feel natural, so you can respond effectively in real-life situations.

Boundary-Setting Statement: Write down a statement of boundary-setting you can use when confronted with an adult tantrum. It might be as simple as saying, "I understand you're upset, but I won't engage in this conversation until we're both calm." Keep it clear and direct. The next time you encounter a tantrum, try saying it out loud and notice how it impacts the interaction.

Emotional Detachment Exercise: Think of a past situation where you were emotionally triggered by someone's tantrum. Close your eyes and imagine yourself observing the situation from a distance, as if you're watching a movie. Picture yourself staying calm, grounded, and unaffected. Journal about how the experience changes when you detach emotionally.

8. The Right Decision Often Feels Wrong
Subchapter Summary

Making decisions, especially those that involve change or stepping into the unknown, can be deeply uncomfortable. Many of us are conditioned to avoid discomfort or second-guess ourselves when faced with difficult choices. In this subchapter, we explore why the right decisions often feel wrong in the moment and how to trust your instincts even when fear, doubt, and uncertainty cloud your judgment. This chapter encourages readers to embrace the discomfort that comes with making bold, life-altering decisions and recognize that these feelings are often a sign of growth, not a warning. We discuss how to make decisions from a place of empowerment, not fear, and how to quiet the inner critic that thrives on self-doubt. By learning to sit with discomfort and develop resilience, you can make decisions that lead to a more authentic, fulfilling life.

5 Key Lessons

Discomfort is a Sign of Growth: When we push ourselves to make decisions that challenge the status quo or push us outside of our comfort zones, discomfort is a natural part of the process. The key is to recognize that feeling uneasy doesn't mean you're making the wrong choice—it often signals that you're moving in the right direction.

The Fear of Making the Wrong Decision Often Stops Us from Making Any Decision: Many people get stuck in analysis paralysis because they fear making the wrong choice. However, the truth is that staying stagnant or avoiding decisions altogether often leads to more regret. Taking action, even with some uncertainty, is a powerful step toward clarity.

Trust Your Intuition, Not Just Your Logic: Logical reasoning is important, but intuition can be just as valuable when making decisions. Trusting your gut helps you tune into your deeper desires and values, even when the decision doesn't appear to be the "right" one on paper.

Decisions are Not Final: One of the biggest fears in decision-making is the thought that once you choose, there's no turning back. However, life is fluid, and most decisions can be adjusted or revisited as new information comes in. Trust that you have the ability to course-correct as needed.

The Right Decision Aligns with Your Values: The "right" decision is one that reflects your values, even if it doesn't always align with others' expectations or conventional wisdom. It's important to ask yourself whether the choice you're making brings you closer to living authentically and in alignment with your truth.

4 Self-Reflection Questions

Think about a decision you've made in the past that felt wrong at the time but turned out to be right. What discomfort did you experience, and how did you overcome it?

When you're facing a difficult decision now, what fear or doubt arises? How can you separate those feelings from the actual impact of the decision?

In what areas of your life do you often second-guess your choices? How can you start trusting your intuition more in those areas?

___
___
___
___
___
___
___
___
___
___
___
___
___
___

Reflect on a recent decision you made that you regret. What lessons did you learn from that choice, and how can you apply them to future decisions?

Life-Changing Exercises

Comfort Zone Expansion Exercise: Make a list of decisions you've avoided making due to fear or discomfort. Pick one that you feel ready to address and make a plan to take action on it. Notice how you feel before, during, and after the decision-making process. Reflect on how the discomfort shifts as you move forward.

Fear-Assessment Practice: The next time you feel torn between two decisions, take a moment to evaluate the fears attached to each option. Ask yourself: What's the worst that could happen? What's the best that could happen? This exercise can help you recognize that fear often amplifies the stakes, and the reality of making a decision is rarely as dire as it seems.

Intuition Journal: Begin a daily journal practice where you write about decisions you're facing and how they feel in your body. Before you analyze or rationalize, note any gut feelings or instincts you experience. Over time, you'll begin to recognize patterns and develop greater confidence in trusting your intuition.

Reframe a "Wrong" Decision: Think about a decision you regret. Instead of focusing on the negative aspects, reframe it by identifying any positive outcomes or lessons that came from it. This exercise will help you see that no decision is truly "wrong"—it's all part of the learning process.

Overcoming Chronic Comparison

9. Yes, Life Isn't Fair
Subchapter Summary

Life is inherently unfair. This simple truth often causes frustration, resentment, and confusion, especially when we compare ourselves to others or feel like we've been dealt a poor hand. In this subchapter, we explore how accepting life's unfairness can actually be liberating. Instead of focusing on the injustices and comparing our lives to others', we'll learn how to shift our perspective and take back control. By acknowledging that life isn't fair, we free ourselves from the constant need for fairness, allowing us to focus on creating our own meaning and finding peace within ourselves. We'll also discuss how we can use the unfairness of life as motivation to shape our own destiny, pursue our goals, and focus on what truly matters to us, rather than seeking validation or equal treatment from external sources.

5 Key Lessons

Life's Unfairness is Universal: Everyone faces challenges, and no one has it all figured out. Life is inherently unfair, but rather than feeling bitter or resentful, embracing this reality allows us to stop searching for perfection or a perfect set of circumstances and begin creating our own path, regardless of the obstacles.

Comparing Yourself to Others Only Increases Suffering: When we compare our journey to someone else's, we miss the beauty of our own unique experiences. Learning to focus on your personal growth and path helps to remove the pressure of living up to someone else's expectations and allows for greater fulfillment.

Fairness is a Social Construct: While fairness can be an ideal in society, it's not something we can control. The more we chase fairness, the more we lose sight of what we can actually control—our thoughts, actions, and how we respond to situations. Releasing the need for fairness opens up space for peace and action.

Success is Built on Resilience, Not Equality: Life doesn't always give us equal opportunities or outcomes. However, resilience—the ability to adapt, learn from challenges, and continue moving forward—is the true measure of success. Resilience allows us to turn setbacks into stepping stones and continue pursuing what matters most.

Empower Yourself by Focusing on What You Can Control: Instead of trying to change the unfairness of life, empower yourself by focusing on what you can control: your mindset, actions, and choices. Taking responsibility for your own growth and happiness will set you free from the resentment that often comes from expecting life to be fair.

4 Self-Reflection Questions

When has life felt unfair to you, and how did you respond to that unfairness? What lessons did you learn from that experience?

In what areas of your life do you find yourself constantly comparing yourself to others? How can you shift your focus to your own growth and goals?

Reflect on a situation where you've felt resentful about not being treated fairly. How could you reframe that situation to focus on what you can control or change?

What is one area of your life where you're still seeking fairness or validation from others? How can you begin to release that need and focus on your personal growth instead?

Life-Changing Exercises

The Unfairness Journal: Begin a journal practice where you reflect on the areas of your life that feel unfair. For each entry, write about how you've responded to that unfairness and how you could reframe the situation to focus on your own growth. This exercise helps you move from frustration to empowerment by shifting the narrative in your mind.

Comparison Detox: Over the next week, notice when you start comparing yourself to others. Each time this happens, pause and write down what you were comparing and why it matters. Then, write a few sentences about how you can refocus on your own unique journey and the things that truly matter to you. This exercise helps you break the cycle of comparison.

Resilience Focus: Think about a recent setback or failure. Instead of focusing on what went wrong, write down how you can learn from it and what steps you can take to bounce back stronger. Use this practice to build resilience and learn to see challenges as opportunities for growth.

Control Circle Exercise: Draw two circles on a piece of paper. Label one circle "Things I Can Control" and the other "Things I Can't Control." In the larger circle, write down everything in your life that you have no power over. In the smaller circle, list what you can control—your actions, your responses, your mindset. This exercise will help you focus on taking responsibility for what's within your control, freeing you from the constant struggle with external factors.

10. How to Make Comparison Your Teacher
Subchapter Summary

Comparison is often seen as a source of frustration, insecurity, and self-doubt. It can leave us feeling less-than, disconnected from our own path, or caught in a cycle of envy. But what if we could use comparison as a tool for personal growth? In this subchapter, we'll explore how to shift your mindset and turn comparison into a powerful teacher. Instead of seeing others' success as a reflection of our inadequacies, we'll learn to view it as a source of inspiration and valuable lessons. By understanding the root of our comparisons and learning to reframe them, we can transform feelings of jealousy and self-doubt into motivation and empowerment. This shift not only helps you grow but also leads to a deeper sense of self-acceptance and confidence, freeing you from the trap of constant comparison.

5 Key Lessons

Comparison is a Natural Human Response: It's natural to compare ourselves to others, but it's important to recognize that these thoughts don't define our self-worth. The key is to use them as a mirror to reflect on your own values, desires, and goals. Comparison doesn't need to be a negative experience—it can be a stepping stone for deeper self-awareness.

What Triggers Your Comparison? Understanding the specific triggers that lead to comparison can help you manage these feelings. Are you comparing your career to others' success? Are you comparing your body to societal standards? By identifying these triggers, you can stop and consciously choose to reframe them in a way that empowers you.

Use Comparison as a Source of Inspiration: Rather than viewing others' success as something you lack, see it as an opportunity to learn. What are they doing that you admire? What strategies can you implement into your own life to help you grow? Use comparison as a springboard for action, not a reason to stay stuck in feelings of inadequacy.

Comparison Shows What You Truly Want: If you're comparing yourself to someone in a particular area, it's a clue about what you truly desire. Is it their confidence, their career, their relationships, or their sense of peace? Recognizing what you admire in others allows you to get clear on your own goals and how you can take actionable steps toward achieving them.

You Are on Your Own Unique Journey: Everyone's path is different. The timing, challenges, and opportunities you face are unique to your life. Constantly comparing yourself to others only detracts from your personal journey. By embracing your individuality, you can focus on building the life that truly reflects your authentic self, free from the need for external validation.

4 Self-Reflection Questions

When you catch yourself comparing to others, what feelings arise? Are they feelings of inadequacy, jealousy, or inspiration? How can you reframe these feelings into a source of motivation?

Think of someone you often compare yourself to. What aspects of their life do you admire? What do those qualities reveal about what you truly want for yourself? How can you start incorporating those elements into your life?

How does comparison influence your self-worth? Do you find yourself feeling "less than" when you compare? What would it take for you to start viewing comparison as a tool for growth, rather than as a reason to feel inadequate?

Reflect on a moment when comparison led to positive change in your life. What did you learn from the experience? How did it motivate you to take action or shift your mindset?

Life-Changing Exercises

The Comparison Reframe Exercise: The next time you find yourself comparing to someone, pause and reflect on what exactly you're comparing. Write down the specific qualities, achievements, or traits you're focusing on. Now, reframe this comparison by asking yourself: "What can I learn from this person?" List 3 things you can apply to your own life to foster growth. This exercise helps you shift your focus from negativity to inspiration and actionable steps.

The Admiration List: Write down the names of 5 people you admire. For each person, list 3 qualities or accomplishments that you admire. Then, reflect on how these qualities can become part of your own personal journey. This exercise helps you recognize the traits you value and how to cultivate them in your own life.

The Comparison Journal: Start a journal specifically for moments when you compare yourself to others. For each entry, write about what sparked the comparison and how it made you feel. Then, write about how you can turn this comparison into something positive—what lessons can you learn from it, and how can you use it to propel you forward? This helps you reframe your thoughts and turn comparison into a learning opportunity.

Visualization of Your Own Success: Take a few minutes to visualize your own path to success. Imagine yourself achieving your goals and living a life that truly reflects your desires and values. Write down what success looks like for you, and what steps you need to take to get there. This exercise reinforces the importance of your unique journey and helps you focus on your goals instead of others' accomplishments.

Part Three: Your Relationships and The Let Them Theory

Mastering Adult Friendship

11. The Truth No One Told You About Adult Friendship

Subchapter Summary

Adult friendships often look very different from what we expected as kids. In childhood, friendships were often simple—based on proximity, shared interests, or just a mutual desire to have fun. But as we grow older, maintaining friendships becomes more complicated. Between busy schedules, career demands, family responsibilities, and personal growth, it's easy to feel disconnected, misunderstood, or even isolated. Yet, adult friendships are essential to our well-being and happiness. In this subchapter, we will uncover the truth about adult friendships: they require effort, understanding, and vulnerability. We will explore why it's hard to maintain close connections as adults, how to prioritize meaningful relationships, and how to let go of friendships that no longer serve your growth. You will learn that true friendship isn't about quantity, but quality, and how nurturing a few deep, supportive relationships can bring more fulfillment than dozens of shallow ones. It's time to reframe your approach to adult friendships, making them a source of strength and support rather than stress or disappointment.

5 Key Lessons

Friendships Require Effort, But They Shouldn't Be a Burden: While relationships take time and energy to build, they should uplift you, not drain you. Recognizing the difference between friendships that energize you and those that feel like obligations is key. Real friendship is mutual and balanced, where both people give and receive support.

Adult Friendships Need Clear Boundaries: As we grow older, it's important to set clear boundaries with our friends. Time constraints, emotional energy, and personal priorities change, and setting healthy limits allows you to nurture your friendships without feeling overwhelmed or resentful. Boundaries help ensure your relationships remain respectful and fulfilling.

It's Okay to Outgrow Friendships: Not all friendships are meant to last forever. As we evolve, so do our needs, values, and interests. Some friendships naturally fade as they no longer align with who we are or where we're going. Letting go of these relationships can feel difficult, but it's necessary for your growth and peace of mind.

Quality Over Quantity: In adulthood, it's not about having a wide circle of friends; it's about having a few close, supportive people who truly understand and care for you. True friendships are built on trust, honesty, and deep connection. Focusing on quality relationships rather than trying to keep up with a large social circle can provide more fulfillment.

Vulnerability is the Key to Connection: It's easy to hide behind a facade, especially when we fear judgment or rejection. However, real friendship is built on vulnerability and openness. The more you allow yourself to be authentic and share your true feelings, the stronger and more meaningful your friendships will be. Authenticity creates deeper connections and fosters trust.

4 Self-Reflection Questions

Reflect on your current friendships. Which ones make you feel supported and understood? Which ones feel draining or one-sided? How can you nurture the relationships that bring you joy and set boundaries with those that are taking more than they give?

Have you ever outgrown a friendship? How did you feel about the process of letting go? What did you learn from that experience, and how did it affect your personal growth?

Are there any friendships in your life where you're not being fully authentic? What's holding you back from being vulnerable, and what would happen if you allowed yourself to show up more honestly?

How do you currently balance your personal needs and obligations with your friendships? Is there space in your life for deeper, more meaningful connections, or do you feel stretched thin by trying to maintain too many relationships?

Life-Changing Exercises

The Friendship Audit: Take time to evaluate your current friendships. Write down the names of your closest friends and assess the quality of each relationship. Are these friendships mutual, supportive, and nourishing, or do they feel like burdens? What are the key characteristics of the friendships that truly fulfill you? This exercise will help you identify where to invest your time and energy.

Create Your Friendship Boundaries: Think about the boundaries you need to set in order to maintain healthy friendships. These can include boundaries around time (e.g., how often you meet), emotional availability, and expectations for communication. Write these boundaries down and have open conversations with your friends about them. This helps ensure your relationships remain balanced and respectful.

The "Letting Go" Letter: Write a letter (you don't have to send it) to a friend or group of friends that you've outgrown. Express your feelings, acknowledging the memories and the role they played in your life. Then, let go of any guilt or resentment associated with moving on. This exercise allows you to release any emotional weight tied to past friendships.

Vulnerability Challenge: Challenge yourself to be vulnerable with one of your close friends. Share something personal you've been holding back, whether it's a fear, an aspiration, or a difficult experience. Notice how it feels to be open and authentic, and observe how this impacts your connection. This exercise encourages deeper bonds and can help you strengthen your emotional intimacy with others.

12. Why Some Friendships Naturally Fade
Subchapter Summary

Not all friendships are meant to last forever, and that's okay. Over time, people change—sometimes subtly, sometimes drastically—and as we evolve, our relationships need to evolve with us. Friendships that once felt deep and meaningful may gradually lose their spark as our lives take different paths. In this subchapter, we'll explore why some friendships naturally fade and why this isn't a failure or a loss but an essential part of our personal growth. The truth is, as we grow older, we often outgrow certain relationships, especially if they no longer align with our values, needs, or life goals. Learning to recognize when a friendship is no longer serving you, and accepting its natural end, is key to maintaining emotional well-being and making space for relationships that truly align with who we are becoming. You'll learn how to release these friendships gracefully and without guilt, honoring the role they played in your life while making room for new, healthier connections.

5 Key Lessons

People Change, and So Do Friendships: As we move through different stages of life, our interests, values, and priorities shift. Friendships that once felt vital may begin to feel less fulfilling as we change. Understanding that it's natural for relationships to ebb and flow helps alleviate the guilt or sadness that can accompany the fading of certain friendships.

Outgrowing Friendships Isn't a Personal Failure: When a friendship fades, it's not a reflection of personal failure or inadequacy. It's simply a sign that your paths are no longer aligned. Allowing relationships to run their course is a sign of maturity and self-awareness, not abandonment.

Recognize When You've Outgrown a Friendship: Identifying when a friendship has run its course can be difficult, especially if the relationship is long-standing. Signs may include feeling drained after interactions, a lack of emotional resonance, or a sense of distance that doesn't feel temporary. Acknowledging these signs is the first step toward acceptance and moving forward.

It's Okay to Let Go Without Bitterness: Ending a friendship doesn't have to be dramatic or negative. Often, the best approach is to let the relationship fade naturally, without resentment or bitterness. By releasing the friendship with understanding, you preserve the good memories and the lessons it brought into your life.

Make Space for New Relationships: When one friendship fades, it creates space for new ones. Embrace the opportunity to form deeper, more aligned connections with people who reflect the person you are becoming. Letting go of past friendships can be the first step toward inviting new, more fulfilling relationships into your life.

4 Self-Reflection Questions

Reflect on a friendship that has naturally faded in your life. How did you feel about the process of letting go? What lessons did you learn from that experience about your own growth and the role that friendship played in your life?

Are there any friendships you currently maintain out of obligation or guilt? How do these relationships make you feel—drained, inspired, conflicted? What might happen if you allowed these friendships to fade naturally?

What qualities do you value most in a friendship now, compared to when you were younger? How have your needs and expectations of friendships shifted over time?

Can you identify any friendships in your life that are no longer serving your personal growth? How can you navigate these relationships with grace, allowing them to fade without regret or emotional turmoil?

Life-Changing Exercises

The Friendship Re-evaluation: Take a moment to reflect on the friendships in your life. Write down the names of your closest friends, and assess how each one aligns with your current values and life goals. Are these relationships still fulfilling, or do you find yourself feeling emotionally drained or disconnected? Use this exercise to evaluate which friendships might be naturally fading and consider how you can honor their end.

Release with Compassion: Think about a friendship that is fading or has ended. Write a letter (which you do not have to send) expressing your gratitude for the relationship, acknowledging the positive experiences you shared, and gently releasing it without regret. Allow yourself to mourn any loss, but also acknowledge the space it opens for new connections. This exercise fosters emotional closure and peace.

Visualize the Space for New Connections: Imagine your life without the fading friendships that no longer serve you. What does that make room for? Visualize the type of friendships you want to create moving forward. What qualities do these new friendships embody? What will they bring into your life? This visualization helps shift your focus from loss to opportunity, making space for more fulfilling relationships.

Set Intentional Friendship Goals: Think about the kind of friendships you want to cultivate in your life moving forward. Are you seeking deeper connections with fewer people? Do you want to prioritize friends who support your growth? Write down three intentional actions you can take in the next month to foster these types of relationships.

13. How to Create the Best Friendships of Your Life
Subchapter Summary

Friendships are some of the most valuable relationships we experience in life, yet creating and maintaining deep, fulfilling connections can feel challenging, especially when juggling other responsibilities. This subchapter offers insight into what it takes to create lasting, meaningful friendships that align with who you are now and who you're becoming. It explores how to build relationships that nourish your soul, support your growth, and provide a sense of belonging. By focusing on authenticity, vulnerability, and mutual respect, you'll learn how to attract and nurture friendships that enrich your life rather than drain it. Creating the best friendships requires intention, a willingness to grow together, and the courage to be real—no masks, no pretenses. The steps outlined here will help you establish bonds that stand the test of time and help you cultivate friendships that truly bring out the best in you.

5 Key Lessons

Authenticity is the Key to Meaningful Connections: The best friendships are rooted in authenticity. Being yourself, without the pressure of meeting expectations or wearing masks, creates a strong foundation for trust and mutual understanding. When both parties are free to be vulnerable and share their true selves, the friendship becomes genuine and unshakeable.

Quality Over Quantity: Having a large circle of friends might seem appealing, but the best friendships are often few and deeply connected. Focus on cultivating relationships with people who understand you, value you, and support your growth. A handful of meaningful friendships will always outweigh many shallow ones.

Friendships Require Effort from Both Sides: While it's important to attract people who align with your values, you also have to put in the effort to maintain and nurture those relationships. Communication, consistency, and showing up for each other are the cornerstones of great friendships. It's a two-way street.

Mutual Respect and Boundaries are Essential: Healthy friendships are based on respect—respect for each other's time, values, boundaries, and individual journeys. A great friendship doesn't involve sacrificing your own needs to please the other person. Setting and honoring boundaries ensures that the relationship remains balanced and fulfilling for both parties.

Embrace the Power of Shared Growth: A great friendship isn't just about supporting each other through the ups and downs. It's about growing together. Whether that's encouraging each other's goals, sharing new ideas, or holding each other accountable for personal development, true friends help each other level up in life.

4 Self-Reflection Questions

When was the last time you felt completely yourself in a friendship? What about that connection made you feel comfortable and authentic? How can you bring more of that into your current relationships?

Reflect on the friendships you have now. Are there any that feel more like obligations than genuine connections? What qualities do you seek in a friend, and are you currently nurturing relationships with those who align with those values?

How do you show up for your friends when they need support? Do you communicate openly and without judgment? Think about the balance of effort in your friendships—are you giving as much as you are receiving?

Are there any boundaries in your friendships that you're not honoring or communicating clearly? How can you assertively, yet compassionately, establish those boundaries to create more harmonious, balanced relationships?

Life-Changing Exercises

Authenticity Check: Take a moment to assess your current friendships. Write down how authentic you feel in each one. Are there any areas where you feel you have to hide or downplay parts of yourself? Make a list of things you could do to bring more of your true self into these relationships, and take one small step this week toward sharing more openly with a friend.

Friendship Vision Board: Create a vision board that represents the type of friendships you want to cultivate. Include images, words, or symbols that reflect the qualities and values you want in your close connections—trust, support, honesty, shared growth, etc. Use this vision board as a reminder of the kind of friendships you deserve and attract into your life.

Friendship Audit: Write down the names of your closest friends, and ask yourself the following questions for each:

- Does this person support my personal growth?
- Do I feel safe and accepted when I'm with them?
- Do we share common values and interests?
- How do I show up for them, and how do they show up for me?

Evaluate each relationship and determine where you can invest more effort to deepen the connection or decide if some relationships need to be redefined or let go.

Intentional Reach-Out: Choose one person you'd like to develop a deeper friendship with and reach out to them with a specific plan—whether it's to schedule a one-on-one meetup, send a thoughtful message, or support them in a personal goal they're pursuing.

Motivating Other People to Change

14. People Only Change When They Feel Like It
Subchapter Summary

This subchapter challenges the common belief that we can change others through force, persuasion, or constant effort. It dives into the reality that true, lasting change in people only occurs when they decide to change for themselves, and not because of external pressure. Understanding this concept is crucial for anyone feeling frustrated or helpless in their relationships, especially when trying to influence someone's behavior or mindset. It also offers a healthy perspective on what we can control—our reactions, boundaries, and decisions—and encourages readers to release the burden of trying to fix or change others. Letting go of this expectation not only eases emotional stress but also opens the door for personal growth and healthier relationships.

5 Key Lessons

Change Must Be Self-Driven: People only change when they are ready to, and not before. No amount of persuasion or encouragement can force someone to change if they're not internally motivated. This lesson invites readers to accept that they cannot control others' decisions, but they can control how they respond to them.

You Can't Fix Anyone: Trying to "fix" or "save" someone can lead to frustration and disappointment. Each person is responsible for their own growth, and as much as we may want to help, we must respect their personal journey. It's important to focus on offering support, not control.

Letting Go Frees You: When you stop trying to change others, you free yourself from the emotional toll of feeling responsible for their transformation. This lesson highlights the power of setting boundaries and letting go of the need to "fix" others, which ultimately benefits both parties.

You Can't Force Growth: Change is a deeply personal experience that requires the individual to recognize their own issues and choose to take action. This lesson teaches that growth doesn't happen under pressure—it happens through self-awareness and personal willingness.

Self-Focus is Key: Instead of focusing on others' flaws or shortcomings, shift the focus to your own growth. By working on yourself, you model the kind of behavior you wish to see, and may even inspire change in others indirectly, through your own example.

4 Self-Reflection Questions

Reflect on a time when you tried to change someone's behavior. How did that experience make you feel, and what was the outcome? What would have happened if you had accepted them as they were instead of trying to change them?

Are there any relationships in your life where you feel the pressure to change someone? How can you let go of this burden and focus on your own actions and growth instead?

How do you feel about your own personal growth? Are there areas in your life where you're waiting for someone else to change in order for you to move forward? How can you shift the focus back to your own journey?

When faced with someone else's resistance to change, how can you support them without pushing them? Reflect on how you can create a space for them to evolve on their own terms, while still maintaining healthy boundaries for yourself.

Life-Changing Exercises

Acceptance Journal: Spend a few minutes each day writing about areas in your life where you've tried to change others. Reflect on how this has impacted you emotionally and mentally. How might your life change if you let go of the need to change others? After a week, read through your reflections and identify any patterns or insights that stand out.

Boundaries Exercise: Identify someone in your life that you feel the urge to "fix" or change. Write down the specific behaviors or attitudes you wish would change. Then, write down ways in which you can shift your focus to your own actions, needs, and boundaries. Practice letting go of the expectation that they need to change for you to feel at peace.

Focus on Your Own Growth: Make a list of areas in your life where you're ready to grow—whether it's personal habits, career goals, or emotional well-being. Set one small goal this week that focuses on your own self-improvement, without trying to influence or change anyone else's actions. Track your progress and celebrate the steps you take.

Change Perspective Activity: Think of a person in your life who has resisted change. Instead of seeing this resistance as a problem, reframe it as a part of their own process. Consider how you can support them in a way that respects their autonomy, while still protecting your own emotional well-being. How can you create a healthier dynamic between you two?

15. Unlock the Power of Your Influence
Subchapter Summary

In this subchapter, we explore the power of personal influence and how you can harness it to improve your life and relationships, without resorting to manipulation or control. Influence doesn't come from overpowering others—it comes from leading by example, setting boundaries, and embodying the values you believe in. Many readers struggle with feeling unheard or invisible, especially when they feel pressure to please or conform to others. This lesson encourages readers to recognize the natural influence they already possess, and shows them how to cultivate it by focusing on authenticity, self-assurance, and emotional intelligence. By recognizing the strength of their personal presence, they can navigate relationships with greater confidence and ease, while inspiring change without needing to force it.

5 Key Lessons

Influence Comes From Authenticity: Your greatest power comes when you show up as your true self. Influence isn't about manipulation; it's about being so grounded in your beliefs and actions that others are naturally drawn to follow your example. People respond to authenticity, and by embracing who you are, you become a source of inspiration for others.

Set Boundaries to Amplify Influence: The more clearly you communicate your boundaries, the more power you give to your influence. When you are able to stand firm in your values and limits, you create respect and understanding in your relationships, allowing you to have a greater impact without sacrificing your well-being.

Influence Is a Ripple Effect: True influence starts small, often within yourself. The way you carry yourself, handle challenges, and interact with others sends ripples through your environment. Even if you're not actively trying to lead, your energy and choices can inspire those around you. Recognize the impact you already have.

Embrace Emotional Intelligence: Understanding and managing your emotions—and those of others—enhances your ability to influence. By honing your emotional intelligence, you become more attuned to others' needs and feelings, allowing you to respond with empathy and clarity. This builds stronger connections and increases your influence in a positive way.

You Don't Need Permission to Lead: Many readers hesitate to use their influence because they feel like they need permission or approval. The truth is, your influence is not dependent on others' validation. Lead from where you are, and understand that your voice, your decisions, and your actions have the power to inspire change—even without explicit approval.

4 Self-Reflection Questions

Reflect on a time when you successfully influenced someone, whether in your personal life or career. What was the outcome, and how did you feel during the process? What did your actions reflect about your own values and beliefs?

How do you currently show up in your relationships and environments? Are you aligning with your true self, or do you feel like you're compromising to gain approval? What steps can you take to be more authentic in how you express yourself?

When you think about your boundaries, how clearly do you communicate them to others? How could setting firmer boundaries enhance your personal influence and create more respect in your relationships?

What is your relationship with emotional intelligence? Reflect on how well you understand your own emotions, as well as those of others. How can you improve your emotional awareness to enhance your influence and create more meaningful connections?

Life-Changing Exercises

Authenticity Check-In: For the next week, pay attention to moments when you feel you're acting in a way that isn't true to yourself—whether it's in a conversation, at work, or in social situations. Journal about these moments and what might have influenced you to act differently than you would have liked. Afterward, consider how you can align your actions more closely with your true self moving forward.

Boundary Setting Practice: Identify one area in your life where you struggle to maintain boundaries. Whether it's with family, friends, or coworkers, practice setting a clear boundary this week. Write down the response you received, how you felt before and after, and what this experience taught you about your personal power.

Ripple Effect Exercise: Take a moment to reflect on how your energy and actions influence those around you, even without direct interaction. Whether it's the way you manage your time, handle stress, or approach tasks, think about how these behaviors can inspire or affect others. This week, focus on a positive action you can take that will ripple out and inspire others to do the same.

Emotional Intelligence Journaling: Start a daily practice of checking in with your emotions and the emotions of others in your immediate environment. Each day, write down one moment where you either effectively used emotional intelligence to connect with someone, or a moment where you missed an opportunity to do so. Reflect on how these moments affected your influence and what you can do next time to improve.

Helping Someone Who is Struggling

16. The More You Rescue, the More They Sink
Subchapter Summary

In this subchapter, we confront a common yet often misunderstood dynamic: the more you try to rescue others, the more they may become reliant on you and less capable of standing on their own. This chapter delves into the consequences of over-rescuing and why it's essential to allow others to face their challenges. For readers who struggle with the urge to help others at the cost of their own well-being, this chapter offers clarity on how enabling behaviors can prevent true growth and healing for both themselves and those they care about. It addresses the frustration of feeling responsible for others' problems, especially when that responsibility drains them emotionally and mentally. The goal of this lesson is to empower readers to step back, release the need to fix everything, and support others in a way that fosters independence and growth. It's about learning the balance between support and overextension, and understanding that true help often involves letting others navigate their own journey.

5 Key Lessons

Rescuing Can Prevent Growth: When you constantly step in to "save" someone, you rob them of the opportunity to face their own challenges and learn from them. Growth happens through overcoming obstacles, not bypassing them. By rescuing others, you inadvertently hinder their personal development.

Over-Rescuing Leads to Dependency: The more you step in to help, the more you may unintentionally reinforce someone's reliance on you. This creates a cycle where the other person expects rescue instead of learning to handle situations themselves, leading to a lack of autonomy and self-sufficiency.

You Can't Control Their Journey: It's natural to want to protect loved ones from pain or failure, but ultimately, you cannot control their path. Allowing people to experience their struggles can teach them resilience and empower them to take control of their own lives. Your role is to support, not to dictate or take over.

Set Boundaries for Your Well-Being: Rescuing others often comes at the expense of your own well-being. By setting clear boundaries, you can prioritize your needs while still offering support when appropriate. This creates a healthier balance in your relationships and helps prevent burnout.

Empathy Over Enabling: While it's important to empathize with those in difficult situations, it's equally important not to enable behaviors that perpetuate helplessness. Supporting others means encouraging them to take responsibility for their actions and choices, not solving their problems for them.

4 Self-Reflection Questions

Think about a time when you tried to rescue someone from a difficult situation. How did that intervention affect their ability to handle future challenges? How did it affect your own well-being and emotional state?

How often do you find yourself stepping in to help others, even when they haven't asked for it? Reflect on how this might create an unhealthy dynamic in your relationships. What are some signs that you may be rescuing others too much?

What boundaries can you set to stop over-rescuing others while still offering meaningful support? How would your life look different if you allowed others to take more responsibility for their problems?

What would happen if you stopped trying to solve everyone's problems and let them face their challenges on their own? How would this impact your sense of self-worth and your relationships?

Life-Changing Exercises

Rescue-Free Week: For the next week, consciously avoid stepping in to fix others' problems, even if it feels uncomfortable. Notice when you feel the urge to rescue and take a step back. Journal about your feelings and the reactions of those around you. What impact did this exercise have on your relationships and personal boundaries?

Empowerment Conversation: Choose someone you've been rescuing and have an honest conversation about your role in their life. Discuss how you can shift from rescuing to supporting. Frame the conversation around empowerment and autonomy, and see how they respond to taking more responsibility for their actions.

Identify Rescue Triggers: Reflect on the specific situations or people that trigger your need to rescue. Are there certain emotional or relational dynamics at play that make you feel responsible for others' challenges? Write down these triggers and brainstorm alternative ways to support without overextending yourself.

Self-Care Commitment: Create a self-care plan that includes time for yourself, free from rescuing others. Schedule time each week to focus solely on your needs and desires. This exercise helps you prioritize yourself without guilt, reinforcing the idea that you cannot give to others if you are running on empty.

17. How to Provide Support the Right Way
Subchapter Summary

Support is essential in any healthy relationship, but providing it in the right way is key to fostering independence, growth, and mutual respect. This chapter explores the concept of offering support without falling into the trap of over-rescuing or enabling. For readers who may struggle with the balance between helping and giving others the space to solve their own problems, this chapter provides the tools to navigate this delicate dynamic. It focuses on how to be a positive influence and an empowering presence in others' lives, without taking on their struggles as your own or sacrificing your well-being in the process. Through this chapter, readers will discover that real support comes from listening, validating feelings, encouraging independence, and offering guidance without taking control. It is about stepping into a role that encourages growth, not one that stifles it.

5 Key Lessons

Support Doesn't Mean Solving Problems: Genuine support involves helping others navigate their issues, not solving them for them. By providing guidance and encouragement, you empower others to find their own solutions, fostering self-reliance and resilience.

Listening Is the Most Powerful Form of Support: Often, people don't need advice as much as they need to be heard. Listening actively without judgment allows others to process their emotions, clarify their thoughts, and feel understood—providing the emotional space they need to work through their challenges.

Encourage, Don't Enable: The difference between supporting someone and enabling them is subtle but important. Support means offering resources, encouragement, and compassion without taking on someone's responsibilities. Enabling means doing things for them that they should be doing for themselves, which can foster dependency and hinder their personal growth.

Set Boundaries While Supporting: Healthy boundaries are crucial when offering support. It's important to recognize when you've given enough, and when to step back. This ensures that you're not sacrificing your own well-being while helping others and prevents feelings of burnout or resentment.

Provide Emotional Support, Not Approval: Support should focus on encouraging others' emotional growth, not on validating their every action. Giving someone the space to explore their feelings and choices helps them grow into their best self, while excessive validation can reinforce insecurity and the need for external approval.

4 Self-Reflection Questions

Think of a recent time when you tried to support someone. Did you find yourself taking on more responsibility than was necessary? How did this affect your relationship and your sense of self?

How do you typically respond when someone confides in you about a problem? Are you more likely to give advice or simply listen? Reflect on how your approach impacts the person you're supporting.

Do you ever feel like you're "fixing" others' problems to avoid facing your own? What can you do to provide support without taking on someone else's challenges as your own?

How can you set healthier boundaries when offering support to others, and what would it feel like to do so without guilt or fear of rejection?

Life-Changing Exercises

Active Listening Practice: Choose a person in your life who often seeks your advice. This week, practice active listening with them. Instead of offering solutions, ask open-ended questions that allow them to explore their feelings and thoughts. Afterward, reflect on how they responded and how this approach felt for you.

Support vs. Enabling Assessment: Make a list of people you feel you provide support to. For each, assess whether you are helping them grow and become more self-reliant or whether you are enabling them by solving their problems for them. Identify one person where you can adjust your approach to foster more independence.

Support Boundaries Journal: Write about a recent situation where you offered support. Did you feel that your boundaries were respected, or did you give more than you could handle? Reflect on how you can set boundaries in similar situations moving forward without feeling guilty.

Self-Care Action Plan: Take a moment to create a self-care plan that balances your personal needs with the support you provide to others. Include boundaries that prevent you from overextending yourself. Prioritize your well-being in this plan and commit to following through for a week.

Choosing the Love You Deserve

18. Let Them Show You Who They Are
Subchapter Summary

One of the hardest truths to accept in relationships is that people will often show us exactly who they are, whether or not it aligns with our expectations or desires. This chapter explores the importance of observing people's actions and words without attempting to change or mold them into something they are not. Letting people show you who they are allows for clarity, healthier boundaries, and deeper understanding. Readers often struggle with the need to "fix" or "save" others, but this approach can lead to disappointment and burnout. The key is to release the urge to control others and instead, learn to observe their behaviors, respect their choices, and make decisions based on what is truly best for you. By doing so, readers can save time and energy while developing healthier, more authentic relationships. This chapter will help you stop projecting your own desires and start embracing people for who they truly are, allowing for a healthier, more peaceful way of connecting.

5 Key Lessons

Actions Speak Louder Than Words: People often tell us who they are through their actions, not their promises. Pay close attention to how they behave in different situations, as this gives you a clearer picture of who they truly are.

You Can't Change People—Only Yourself: While it's natural to want to help or change others, the truth is, people will only change when they are ready. You cannot control or fix someone; the only person you can change is yourself. Accepting this fact frees you from unrealistic expectations and unnecessary frustration.

Setting Boundaries Is Key to Acceptance: When you let people show you who they are, you also need to set boundaries that protect your emotional and mental well-being. Respecting who they are does not mean tolerating behaviors that hurt you. Healthy boundaries allow you to engage in relationships that are mutually respectful and fulfilling.

Trust the Process, Not the Outcome: The people in your life will reveal their true selves over time. Trust that this process of discovery will help you understand who truly aligns with your values, and who you may need to let go of. You don't need to rush or force connections; let them unfold naturally.

Release the Need for Approval: Letting people show you who they are also means releasing the need for approval or validation from others. You are not defined by others' opinions of you, and their behaviors are not a reflection of your worth. By embracing your own identity and accepting others for theirs, you cultivate healthier relationships.

4 Self-Reflection Questions

When someone shows you who they truly are, how do you typically respond? Do you accept them as they are, or do you try to change them? Reflect on a recent situation where someone's behavior didn't align with your expectations—what did you learn from it?

What are your biggest struggles with letting people show you who they are? Is it because you fear disappointment, or do you feel compelled to "fix" things? How can you shift your perspective to embrace people as they are?

How can you tell if someone is showing you who they truly are, versus when they are simply trying to meet your expectations? What signs or behaviors will help you distinguish the two?

Think about a relationship where you've tried to change someone or expected them to act differently. How did this impact your emotional well-being? How can you let go of these expectations and accept people as they are moving forward?

Life-Changing Exercises

Observational Exercise: This week, focus on observing the behaviors and actions of those around you. Notice how they act in different situations (e.g., when they are stressed, when they are happy, when they are upset). Reflect on how their actions align with their words and if there is anything you may have overlooked before. Write down your observations.

Expectation Inventory: Make a list of expectations you have for the people closest to you. For each person, ask yourself: Are these expectations realistic? Are they based on their actions or my desires? What can I let go of to accept them more fully for who they are?

Letting Go of Control: Choose one relationship in your life where you feel the need to "fix" or "change" the other person. Commit to stepping back and allowing them to show you who they are, without interference. Observe how this shift affects the dynamic, and reflect on your feelings during this process.

Boundary Setting Practice: Reflect on a recent situation where someone's behavior caused you distress. Write down the behavior, and then create a boundary that would protect your well-being if it happens again. Practice asserting this boundary in a way that feels respectful but firm.

19. How to Take Your Relationship to the Next Level
Subchapter Summary

Taking a relationship to the next level is often a challenging yet transformative experience. Whether it's deepening a romantic connection, strengthening a friendship, or improving family dynamics, this chapter explores how to move past surface-level interactions and create a relationship that is meaningful, authentic, and long-lasting. Readers often find themselves stuck in stagnant relationships or unsure of how to evolve the dynamics. This chapter emphasizes the importance of open communication, vulnerability, and shared growth. It encourages readers to move beyond fear, self-doubt, and societal expectations, and instead focus on creating connections that align with their true selves. By doing so, readers can establish relationships that provide mutual support, understanding, and respect. It's about moving past transactional connections and building a partnership based on love, trust, and shared purpose.

5 Key Lessons

Vulnerability Is the Bridge to Deeper Connection: The key to deepening any relationship is vulnerability. By opening up, sharing fears, desires, and struggles, both parties can move past superficial interactions and foster a bond that feels real and empowering.

Communication Is the Cornerstone of Growth: Effective communication is the foundation of any relationship that thrives. Expressing needs, expectations, and feelings openly and honestly creates an environment where both people can feel heard, valued, and respected.

Shared Growth Builds Stronger Bonds: Relationships grow when both individuals commit to personal development. Support each other's growth, both individually and as a couple or team, and prioritize each other's well-being. This mutual growth creates a stronger foundation for the future.

You Don't Need to Change Who You Are to Make Someone Else Comfortable: A common struggle for readers is the fear of losing themselves in relationships. It's essential to stay true to your identity while allowing the relationship to evolve. The best relationships are those where both people can show up as their authentic selves without fear of judgment.

Setting Clear, Healthy Boundaries Encourages Deeper Respect: Establishing boundaries is essential for protecting your emotional and mental health while strengthening a relationship. Healthy boundaries allow both parties to feel safe, valued, and respected. They also prevent feelings of resentment and burnout.

4 Self-Reflection Questions

Think about a relationship that you'd like to deepen. What are the current barriers preventing you from moving to the next level? Are they based on fear, insecurity, or miscommunication? How can you address these obstacles?

_____

_____

_____

_____

_____

_____

_____

_____

_____

_____

_____

_____

_____

_____

_____

_____

How open are you with your partner, friend, or family member about your true feelings and needs? Do you feel heard and understood? Reflect on how being more vulnerable could improve your relationship.

In what ways are you supporting the growth of the person you care about? Are you actively encouraging them to pursue their goals and dreams, or are you holding them back? How can you show up as a better supporter?

Are there any boundaries in your relationship that need to be reestablished or reinforced? What are they, and how can you communicate them in a way that is loving yet firm?

Life-Changing Exercises

Vulnerability Challenge: This week, choose one relationship in your life where you feel there is potential to go deeper. Share something personal with that person that you've never discussed before. It could be a fear, a dream, or a struggle you've been dealing with. Observe how it feels to be vulnerable, and reflect on how it affects your connection.

Communication Exercise: Choose a relationship where communication has been lacking or strained. Set aside time for a heart-to-heart conversation. Practice being open, honest, and attentive. Avoid distractions and focus on really listening. Write about how this conversation shifts your connection.

Growth Planning Session: Sit down with the person you want to deepen your relationship with and have a discussion about your mutual goals. What personal goals are you working on? How can you support each other in those goals? What steps can you take together to grow as individuals and as a couple or team?

Boundary Setting Role Play: Reflect on a relationship where you've felt your boundaries were crossed. Write down a situation where you need to set a boundary. Then, role-play how you would assert that boundary in a clear, calm, and respectful way. Practice this with a trusted friend or on your own.

Conclusion

Reflection on the Workbook Journey

As you've journeyed through this workbook, you've explored practical ways to implement the Let Them theory in your life. You've uncovered key insights into managing stress, letting go of unrealistic expectations, and embracing your authentic self. Along the way, you've developed deeper self-awareness, gained confidence in setting boundaries, and learned how to take ownership of your relationships and personal growth.

This workbook was designed to not only guide you through the theoretical aspects of the Let Them mindset but also to provide actionable tools, exercises, and reflections that help you make these ideas a living part of your daily experience. Through each chapter, you've discovered that life is unpredictable, people can be challenging, and not everything is within your control, but ultimately, you hold the power to shape how you respond.

By practicing the lessons shared here, you've taken the first steps in letting go of external expectations and embracing your ability to thrive. You've also learned that it's okay to be imperfect, to face uncertainty, and to recognize that growth comes from taking bold, conscious steps forward.

Final Insights and Next Steps

As you move forward, remember that the journey to full implementation of Let Them is ongoing. There will be moments when old habits creep back in—when you feel the urge to seek validation, when boundaries blur, or when stress feels overwhelming. These are natural, and they're a part of growth. The key is to stay consistent, revisit the exercises and reflections that resonated with you, and continue to embrace the mindset shift you've begun here.

To truly embody the Let Them philosophy in every area of your life, here are some next steps to guide you:

Keep Reflecting: Continue journaling and reflecting on the insights you've gained. You might want to revisit specific chapters when challenges arise, such as dealing with difficult people or feeling overwhelmed by responsibilities. These tools are here to support you long-term.

Take Action Daily: Apply what you've learned by setting small, achievable goals based on the exercises you've completed. Whether it's practicing vulnerability in relationships or asserting a boundary at work, daily actions will create lasting change.

Build a Support System: Surround yourself with like-minded individuals who encourage your growth and honor your boundaries. Find people who understand your journey and are supportive of the principles you're applying in your life.

Celebrate Progress: Acknowledge the small wins. Each step you take towards healthier boundaries, less stress, and more authentic relationships is a victory. Celebrate those moments, as they are the building blocks for greater change.

Embrace Imperfection: Don't expect perfection—just progress. Life will always present challenges, and no one is immune to setbacks. What matters is your ability to keep moving forward with grace and resilience.

By taking the next step in your journey, you will continue to unlock the power of the Let Them mindset, turning it into a transformative force in your life. Keep moving towards a future where you're free from unnecessary stress, external pressures, and the need for approval. The tools you now have will help you not only create healthier relationships but also embrace the fullness of your authentic self.

Your journey doesn't end here—it's just the beginning. Embrace it with confidence and a sense of purpose. The best is yet to come.

Appendix

- Special Applications of The Let Them Theory:

Parenting

Parenting is one of the most challenging and rewarding roles a person can take on, and it's easy to get caught up in the whirlwind of external pressures, societal expectations, and well-meaning advice from others. The Let Them theory can be a transformative tool in parenting, allowing you to foster an environment that prioritizes your child's independence, emotional well-being, and growth while also maintaining your own sense of balance and self-respect.

Subchapter Summary

In this section, we'll explore how the Let Them theory can be applied to parenting by focusing on key principles such as letting your children make their own mistakes, establishing healthy boundaries, and allowing them to experience both success and failure in their own time. You'll learn how to embrace the idea that your children are individuals with their own paths, and how to cultivate an atmosphere where they can thrive without being over-controlled or overly protected.

We'll also look at how to manage your own expectations as a parent, balancing your love and care with the understanding that your child's journey is not yours to control. The goal is to create a partnership in parenting where respect, autonomy, and growth are at the core of your relationship.

5 Key Lessons

Let Them Fail: Failure is a natural part of learning and growth. Allowing your child to face the consequences of their actions, while still offering support, helps them build resilience and problem-solving skills.

Let Them Make Decisions: From a young age, children should be given the space to make choices, whether it's picking out clothes or deciding how to spend their free time. This encourages independence and confidence in their judgment.

Let Them Express Themselves: Embrace the uniqueness of your child's personality. Support their individuality and create a space where they feel safe expressing their emotions, opinions, and ideas without fear of judgment.

Let Them Have Their Own Experiences: While you may want to protect your child from every hardship, real-life experiences—both positive and negative—are essential for growth. Allow them to navigate the world, face challenges, and learn from their experiences.

Let Them Set Boundaries: Teach your children to recognize and set their own boundaries, respecting their own needs and the needs of others. By modeling healthy boundaries, you give them the tools to protect their emotional and mental well-being.

4 Self-Reflection Questions

In what areas of parenting do I tend to overprotect my child, and how can I shift to allowing them more space to grow?

How do I react when my child fails or makes a mistake? What can I do to show support without taking over the situation?

Are there any specific expectations or pressures I place on my child based on my own desires or fears? How can I let go of these to allow them to follow their own path?

How can I encourage my child to express themselves more freely, and what can I do to make them feel heard and respected?

Life-Changing Exercises

Allow Space for Decision-Making: Set aside a week where you actively encourage your child to make decisions on their own, whether it's about their day-to-day activities, choices for family outings, or handling a minor issue. Observe their process, and resist the urge to jump in unless asked for guidance.

Create a "Failure Wall": Set up a place in your home where your child can pin up their mistakes, failures, or things they didn't succeed in right away. Encourage them to reflect on what they learned from each experience and celebrate their perseverance.

Model Boundaries in Action: Choose one area where you need to set a clear boundary (with your child or within the family), and demonstrate the process of setting and respecting that boundary. Teach your child how boundaries can be both healthy and flexible.

Active Listening Practice: Spend dedicated one-on-one time with your child where you focus solely on listening. Practice active listening techniques—mirroring their words, reflecting their emotions, and providing validation without offering solutions unless asked. This builds trust and encourages open communication.

By applying the Let Them theory to parenting, you can nurture a relationship with your child that allows them to grow into their best selves while also giving yourself the space to thrive as an individual. The lessons you've learned here can help you foster an environment of respect, autonomy, and love, ensuring that both you and your child flourish.

Teams

In any team—whether in a professional, sports, or personal context—creating an environment where individuals feel empowered and supported is key to fostering collaboration, creativity, and overall success. The Let Them theory can be incredibly effective in transforming the dynamics of a team by emphasizing trust, autonomy, and mutual respect. By giving team members the space to perform, make mistakes, and own their contributions, you can unlock their full potential and create a thriving, high-performing group.

Subchapter Summary

This section looks into how the Let Them theory can be applied within team settings to maximize productivity, collaboration, and individual growth. We'll discuss how letting team members have the freedom to approach tasks in their own way, make decisions independently, and learn from both their successes and failures fosters a healthy, empowered team culture. Additionally, we'll look at how to balance leadership with autonomy, ensuring that your team feels supported but also trusted to take initiative and make their own choices.

You'll learn how to shift from micromanaging to creating a supportive environment where everyone can thrive, leading to more engaged, confident, and creative team members. We'll also explore how the Let Them theory can help resolve conflicts, foster better communication, and improve team morale.

5 Key Lessons

Let Them Lead: Give team members the opportunity to take charge of projects or initiatives, even if it's outside of their usual role. This builds confidence, fosters leadership skills, and encourages innovation within the team.

Let Them Learn from Mistakes: Avoid stepping in every time someone makes a mistake. Instead, allow your team to learn from their failures and find solutions on their own. This encourages resilience and problem-solving.

Let Them Contribute Freely: Encourage an open environment where every team member can voice their ideas, opinions, and concerns without fear of judgment or rejection. Everyone's perspective adds value.

Let Them Work Independently: Allow individuals to manage their own tasks or projects without constant oversight. Trusting team members to take ownership leads to greater accountability and a sense of pride in their work.

Let Them Reflect: Encourage regular reflection on both individual and team performance. This can help identify areas for growth and improvement while allowing everyone to take responsibility for their own progress.

4 Self-Reflection Questions

How often do I find myself micromanaging my team, and what steps can I take to give them more autonomy?

In what areas of the team do I feel the need to control or direct the outcomes? How can I shift from controlling to empowering?

How do I handle mistakes within the team? What can I do to create a culture where learning from failures is encouraged and celebrated?

Are there opportunities where I can let my team take the lead, and how can I ensure that they have the necessary support to succeed in those situations?

Life-Changing Exercises

Empowerment Challenge: Identify a task or project that you typically manage and give it to a team member to lead. Offer guidance if needed, but resist the urge to take over. Reflect on how it impacts both their growth and the team's dynamics.

Mistake Wall Exercise: Encourage team members to share mistakes they've made (either personally or professionally) and the lessons they learned from them. Create a safe space for discussing failures and turning them into growth opportunities.

Open Idea Sessions: Dedicate time during team meetings to brainstorming or problem-solving sessions where everyone's voice is heard. This can be used to tackle specific challenges or generate new ideas for projects. The goal is to create a space where creativity and collaboration are nurtured.

Autonomy Week: For one week, allow each team member to manage a specific task or aspect of a project on their own. Check in at the end of the week to assess progress, but focus on providing feedback and offering praise for their efforts rather than correcting them.

By embracing the Let Them theory within your team, you can create an environment that fosters creativity, accountability, and growth. When team members feel trusted to take ownership of their work and contribute freely, they are more likely to invest their energy and expertise into achieving collective goals. This approach not only enhances team performance but also builds stronger relationships and trust among team members.

Romantic Relationships

In romantic relationships, maintaining a balance between connection, independence, and mutual respect is crucial for long-term happiness and fulfillment. The Let Them theory offers profound insights into how partners can empower each other, respect boundaries, and grow individually while remaining deeply connected. By embracing the principle of letting your partner be themselves, make their own choices, and learn from their own experiences, you create a relationship dynamic rooted in trust, freedom, and love.

Subchapter Summary

This section explores how the Let Them theory can transform romantic relationships by promoting emotional autonomy, self-discovery, and personal growth for both partners. We'll discuss how letting your partner express themselves freely, pursue their passions, and navigate challenges on their own terms strengthens the relationship. By understanding that true love involves giving your partner the space to be who they are—without imposing your expectations or desires—you create a foundation of mutual respect, trust, and support.

In romantic relationships, the Let Them theory encourages partners to support each other's growth without trying to change or control each other. It's about accepting your partner as they are, allowing them to make mistakes, and trusting that they have the ability to grow and learn independently. We'll also examine how letting go of unrealistic expectations, codependency, and the need to control can lead to healthier, more fulfilling relationships.

5 Key Lessons

Let Them Be Themselves: Embrace your partner's uniqueness without trying to change them. True love is accepting your partner for who they are and celebrating their individuality.

Let Them Pursue Their Own Passions: Support your partner in exploring their hobbies, career, or personal interests. Encouraging independence helps build confidence and prevents feelings of resentment.

Let Them Make Mistakes: Don't rush to fix everything or protect them from failure. Let your partner navigate their own challenges and learn from their experiences, knowing that mistakes are part of growth.

Let Them Take Space: A healthy relationship requires both partners to have time for themselves. Allow your partner to take the space they need to recharge and focus on their personal needs without guilt or judgment.

Let Them Lead in Certain Areas: Empower your partner by allowing them to take the lead in aspects of the relationship, whether it's planning an outing, making decisions, or supporting your growth. This creates a balanced dynamic built on mutual respect.

4 Self-Reflection Questions

How often do I feel the need to change or control my partner? What are the reasons behind these urges, and how can I shift my perspective to embrace their individuality?

Am I allowing enough space for my partner to pursue their passions and interests? How can I better support their personal growth?

Do I have unrealistic expectations of my partner? How can I adjust my expectations to be more in line with reality and their needs?

How do I react when my partner makes mistakes? Am I allowing them the space to learn from these experiences, or do I try to protect them from failure?

Life-Changing Exercises

The Freedom Challenge: For one week, consciously let go of the need to control or change your partner in any way. Allow them to make their own decisions, express themselves freely, and take the lead in certain aspects of your life together. Reflect on how it feels to release control and embrace their autonomy.

Independent Pursuits Exercise: Encourage both you and your partner to spend time exploring a personal passion or interest that doesn't involve each other. Afterward, share your experiences with each other and discuss how it made you feel. This can help foster independence and deepen your connection.

Mistakes Are Learning Opportunities: Next time your partner makes a mistake, resist the urge to fix it or offer immediate solutions. Instead, give them the opportunity to figure it out themselves, while offering support and encouragement. Reflect on how this approach impacts both of you.

Space for Growth: Have a conversation with your partner about how you can both create space for personal growth. This could mean scheduling alone time, supporting each other's goals, or setting boundaries that allow for individual pursuits.

Applying the Let Them theory in romantic relationships can transform how you view each other's autonomy, growth, and mutual respect. When you let your partner be themselves, pursue their passions, and make their own choices, you are building a relationship that is healthy, empowering, and sustainable. By fostering an environment of trust and acceptance, you create the space for both partners to flourish individually and as a couple.

School

In the context of school, the Let Them theory can offer a fresh and empowering perspective for both students and educators. It emphasizes the importance of allowing students to take ownership of their learning, make independent decisions, and develop self-confidence. For educators and parents, it's about creating an environment where students are encouraged to explore their own paths, learn from their mistakes, and grow at their own pace. By letting students take the reins of their educational journey, you foster a sense of responsibility, autonomy, and resilience that can extend far beyond the classroom.

Subchapter Summary

This section explores how the Let Them theory can be applied in school settings to enhance student growth and academic success. By allowing students to take charge of their learning, pursue their interests, and make decisions about their educational path, the theory promotes self-reliance and builds a positive learning environment. Rather than focusing solely on achievement or conformity, Let Them encourages students to embrace their unique learning styles and strengths, leading to more meaningful and personalized educational experiences.

For educators and parents, applying the Let Them theory means providing support, guidance, and encouragement while giving students the freedom to explore, experiment, and learn from their experiences. This approach fosters self-esteem, accountability, and a love for learning that can last a lifetime.

5 Key Lessons

Let Them Explore Their Interests: Encourage students to discover their passions and interests, even if they fall outside traditional academic subjects. Allowing exploration helps students develop a sense of purpose and intrinsic motivation for learning.

Let Them Make Mistakes: Mistakes are essential to learning. Allow students to make errors without fear of judgment, as this leads to growth, critical thinking, and resilience.

Let Them Take Ownership of Their Learning: Give students opportunities to make choices about how they learn, whether through projects, presentations, or exploring topics that interest them. Ownership increases engagement and responsibility.

Let Them Set Goals: Encourage students to set their own academic and personal goals. When students are involved in goal-setting, they become more motivated and focused on their learning journey.

Let Them Lead: Provide students with leadership opportunities within the classroom or school community. Letting them take on leadership roles fosters confidence, communication skills, and the ability to work collaboratively.

4 Self-Reflection Questions

How can I allow students more autonomy in their learning? What are some areas where I can give them more freedom to make choices and explore their interests?

How do I handle mistakes in the classroom? Am I creating an environment where students feel comfortable failing and learning from their mistakes?

Am I giving students enough opportunities to set their own goals? How can I incorporate goal-setting into my classroom or learning environment?

How can I help students develop leadership skills? What opportunities can I create for them to take on leadership roles or responsibilities?

Life-Changing Exercises

Passion Project: Have students create a project around a subject they are passionate about, allowing them to choose the topic and how they present it. Encourage them to research, experiment, and present their findings. This fosters independence, creativity, and ownership of their learning.

Mistake Reflection Exercise: After an error or failure, guide students in reflecting on the mistake and identifying what they learned from it. Encourage them to share how the mistake helped them grow or change their approach.

Goal-Setting Activity: Provide students with a template for setting personal and academic goals. Have them define their goals, break them down into actionable steps, and regularly check in on their progress. This instills a sense of responsibility and self-direction.

Leadership Challenge: Create a classroom or school-wide leadership project where students can volunteer to lead activities, organize events, or take responsibility for specific tasks. Reflect on how this experience builds confidence and teamwork.

Applying the Let Them theory in a school setting helps students develop a sense of ownership over their education, empowers them to make decisions, and teaches them the value of self-reliance and responsibility. For educators, this approach creates a more engaging and supportive environment, fostering creativity, independence, and resilience in students. Letting students lead their own learning path can profoundly impact their academic success and personal development.

Family

When applied within the family dynamic, the Let Them theory encourages a healthier, more balanced relationship between parents, children, and other family members. It promotes the idea that each individual in the family, regardless of age, has the autonomy to make decisions, voice their opinions, and contribute to the household in meaningful ways. For parents, it involves stepping back and giving children the space to grow, make mistakes, and take ownership of their lives while still providing necessary guidance and support.

The Let Them theory also helps in fostering more respectful and harmonious relationships between family members, where each person's needs, emotions, and boundaries are respected. It's about allowing individuals to be themselves, rather than forcing them into roles or expectations, and recognizing that growth within the family happens through mutual respect and trust.

Subchapter Summary

This section delves into how the Let Them theory can be applied within family dynamics to create stronger, more supportive relationships. Whether it's with children, siblings, or parents, Let Them allows individuals to thrive within the family by respecting boundaries, encouraging autonomy, and offering support when needed. Rather than taking control or trying to dictate outcomes, family members are empowered to take charge of their own lives, which in turn creates a more peaceful and nurturing home environment.

The Let Them approach in families encourages open communication, empathy, and the understanding that each family member's path is unique. Parents can embrace their role as guides rather than controllers, and children can feel confident in making decisions and growing into responsible, self-sufficient individuals.

5 Key Lessons

Let Them Make Their Own Choices: Allow children and family members to make decisions about their own lives, from what they eat to how they manage their time. This fosters responsibility and accountability.

Let Them Fail (and Learn from It): Mistakes are a natural part of life. Allowing family members to experience setbacks without stepping in to fix everything teaches resilience and growth.

Let Them Have Their Own Opinions: Respect everyone's individuality and opinions, even when they differ from your own. This creates a more open, accepting family culture where each member feels heard and valued.

Let Them Lead at Home: Give children the opportunity to take on leadership roles in the family, whether it's organizing family activities or helping with household tasks. This builds confidence and a sense of ownership.

Let Them Find Their Own Path: Trust that each family member's journey is unique. Support them in exploring their passions and interests, without imposing your own dreams or expectations on them.

4 Self-Reflection Questions

How often do I allow family members to make their own choices, especially when it comes to their lives or personal interests?

How do I handle mistakes or failures within the family? Do I allow others to learn from their errors, or do I try to fix everything for them?

Am I respecting the individuality and opinions of all family members, especially when they differ from my own?

How can I give my children or family members more opportunities to lead within the household and feel responsible for their roles?

Life-Changing Exercises

Decision-Making Challenge: Give children or family members a small but important decision to make on their own. This could be related to a family activity, meal planning, or how to spend free time. Support them in making the decision, but allow them to take full ownership of the outcome.

Failure Reflection Exercise: After a failure or setback, guide family members in reflecting on what went wrong and what they can learn from the experience. Encourage them to view failure as an opportunity for growth.

Family Leadership Role: Assign family members leadership roles for specific household tasks or events. Allow them to take charge and handle responsibilities with minimal intervention. Reflect on how this boosts their confidence and independence.

Vision Board for Each Family Member: Have each family member create a vision board that represents their personal dreams, goals, and aspirations. Use this as a way to discuss their individual paths and encourage support from others.

By applying the Let Them theory within the family, you create an environment of trust, autonomy, and growth. It's about allowing each person to take ownership of their choices and actions, while still being there to support and guide them when necessary. This leads to stronger family bonds, more meaningful relationships, and the development of well-rounded, self-sufficient individuals. Through mutual respect and understanding, the family can thrive and support each member in becoming the best version of themselves.

Made in the USA
Columbia, SC
06 January 2025